# the asian spicy snack

## charmaine solomon

# book

HAMLYN

First published in Great Britain in 1999 by Hamlyn
an imprint of Reed Consumer Books Limited
Michelin House, 81 Fulham Road
London SW3 6RB
and Auckland and Melbourne

Produced and published in Australia by
New Holland Publishers (Australia) Pty Ltd
Sydney • London • Cape Town

14 Aquatic Drive, Frenchs Forest, NSW 2086,
Australia

24 Nutford Place, London WIH 6DQ
United Kingdom

80 McKenzie Street, Cape Town 8001
South Africa

ISBN 0 600 59731 8

Publishing General Manager: Jane Hazell
Publishers: Clare Coney, Averill Chase
Designer: Guy Mirabella
Design Assistant: Laurence Lemmon-Warde
Styling: Margaret Alcock
Food cooked by: Nina Harris, Jill Pavey
China: Villeroy & Boch, Australia Pty Ltd
Quark Xpress: Melbourne Media Services
Printer: L Rex Printing, China

# contents

# yum cha

# spring rolls

makes 20

250 g (8 oz) pork fillet
250 g (8 oz) raw or cooked prawns
  1 cup bean sprouts
  ½ small Chinese cabbage
  2 tablespoons peanut oil
  1 teaspoon crushed garlic
  1 teaspoon finely grated ginger
  ½ cup finely chopped water
    chestnuts

8 spring onions, chopped
2 tablespoons light soy sauce
  salt to taste
3 teaspoons cornflour
1 teaspoon oriental sesame oil
1 packet frozen spring roll
  wrappers, 12.5 cm (5 inch) size
  peanut oil for deep-frying

Finely chop or mince the pork. Shell and devein prawns then chop them finely. Pinch any straggly ends from the bean sprouts. Finely shred the ribs of the cabbage to give 2 cups. Heat 1 tablespoon oil in the wok and gently fry the garlic and ginger for only a few seconds. Add the pork, turning the heat to high, and cook it, tossing until it changes colour. Add the prawns and fry the mixture for 1 or 2 minutes longer. Remove from wok. Heat remaining tablespoon of oil, add the vegetables and toss them until they are wilted, then add the soy sauce. Cook the mixture, tossing for one further minute. Mix the cornflour with one tablespoon of cold water. Push the food to the side of the wok and stir the blended cornflour into the liquid in the centre. Cook it, stirring until the sauce boils and thickens. Transfer it to a large bowl and leave it to cool.

Place 2 tablespoons of cooled filling along the centre of the bottom edge of each spring roll wrapper and roll it up, turning in the ends to enclose the filling. Moisten the final edge with water and press it to seal. Deep-fry the spring rolls a few at a time in hot oil until they are golden brown. Drain them on paper towels and serve warm.

# Vietnamese spring rolls

makes 50

50 or 60 g (2 oz) bean thread
    vermicelli
2 small onions or 6 spring onions,
    finely chopped
375 g (12 oz) pork mince
250 g (8 oz) crab meat
½ teaspoon salt
¼ teaspoon ground black pepper
25 sheets spring roll pastry,
    21.5 cm (10 inch) size

peanut oil for deep-frying
lettuce leaves, sprigs of mint,
    Vietnamese mint or
    coriander

**Nuoc Cham sauce**
1 lime
2 tablespoons fish sauce
2 tablespoons sugar
    garlic, crushed
    hot chilli

Soak bean thread vermicelli in hot water to cover for 10–15
minutes. Drain it, measure ¾ cup and cut it into short lengths.
Combine it with onions, pork, crab and seasonings.

Form this filling into 50 rolls. Cut the pastry sheets into halves.
Place a quantity of filling on to each sheet, rolling the sheet up,
turning the sides in to enclose the filling. Moisten the edge with
water and place the join downwards to make a seal.

Heat 750 ml (24 fl oz) of peanut oil in a wok or deep frying pan and
cook the spring rolls on medium heat until they are brown, then drain
them. Wrap each roll in lettuce with sprig of mint or coriander. Dip it
in Nuoc Cham sauce made from the juice and pulp of a lime,
2 tablespoons each of fish sauce, water and sugar, a little crushed garlic and
hot chilli, seeded and sliced.

# steamed dumplings

makes about 25

**Chinese dumpling filling**
6 dried shiitake (Chinese) mushrooms
250 g (8 oz) minced pork
250 g (8 oz) raw prawns
½ cup finely chopped spring onions
½ cup chopped canned water chestnuts or canned bamboo shoot
½ teaspoon salt or to taste

1 tablespoon light soy sauce
1 teaspoon oriental sesame oil
peanut oil for deep-frying

**Dumplings**
30 sheets fine egg pastry (see below)
125 g (4 oz) small school prawns, shelled
oriental sesame oil

Soak the mushrooms in very hot water for 30 minutes. Squeeze out any excess liquid, discard the stems and chop the mushroom caps finely. Put the mushrooms and pork into a bowl. Shell, devein and chop the prawns and add to the bowl with the spring onions, water chestnuts or bamboo shoot, salt, soy sauce and sesame oil. Mix these ingredients until combined.

Put heaped teaspoons of filling on each square of pastry and gather the pastry around the filling, leaving the top open like a little drawstring purse. On top of each put a small prawn, pressing it down firmly on the filling. Brush strips of greaseproof paper with sesame oil and place them in the steamer. Arrange the dumplings on the oiled paper strips and steam them over boiling water for 15–20 minutes. Serve warm with soy sauce or chilli sauce for dipping.

If you are unable to buy the fine egg (wonton) pastry, here's how to make it. Sift 2 cups of plain flour and ½ teaspoon salt into a bowl. Beat one egg with 125 ml (4 fl oz) of water, add this to the sifted flour and mix it well. Knead the dough for 10 minutes, then cover and leave it aside for 30 minutes. Divide the dough into four. Roll each portion on a floured surface until it is very thin. Cut 8 cm (3 inch) squares and dust them with cornflour to prevent sticking when they are stacked. Wrap the pastry sheets in plastic and store them in the refrigerator for up to a few days until required.

# mini
spring rolls

2 tablespoons peanut oil
2 cups Chinese cabbage stems,
   finely shredded
3 teaspoons cornflour
8 sheets spring roll pastry, 25 cm
   (10 inch) size
   peanut oil for deep-frying
   Chinese dumpling filling (see
   page 6)

Heat the peanut oil in a wok and fry the dumpling filling until it is no longer pink. Add the cabbage stems and continue cooking for a few minutes, until the stems are tender but still crisp. Mix the cornflour with a tablespoon of cold water and stir it into the liquid collected in the wok until it has boiled and thickened. Turn the mixture into a large bowl and leave it to cool.

Cut each sheet of spring roll pastry into 4 squares. Place a teaspoonful of the filling near one end and roll the pastry up around it, turning in the sides of the pastry to enclose the filling. Moisten the last edge with water and place the join downwards. When all the rolls are made they may be covered and refrigerated until close to serving time, then fried a few at a time in hot oil until they are golden brown all over (about 2 minutes). Drain them on paper towels and serve warm.

# pearl balls

makes 30

1 cup glutinous rice
1 quantity Chinese dumpling
    filling, using 500 g (1 lb) pork
    instead of prawns (see page 6)
1 egg, beaten

Soak the rice in cold water to cover for 2 hours, then drain and spread it on paper towels.

Prepare the filling, adding beaten egg. Form the filling into balls with wet hands, and roll each ball in the rice, pressing firmly. Put the balls on a lightly oiled steamer rack and steam them over boiling water for 30 minutes, adding more boiling water as it reduces. Serve the balls warm with a dipping sauce, such as soy or chilli, or if a sweeter sauce is preferred, bottled plum sauce.

# cloud swallows

*These tiny savoury dumplings are made with wonton wrappers. The picturesque name comes from the points of the pastry which represent the beak and wings of a little swallow.*

**makes about 20**

6 **dried shiitake mushrooms**
375 **g (12 oz) raw prawns**
½ **cup of finely chopped canned bamboo shoots**
4 **spring onions, finely chopped**
250 **g (8 oz) minced pork**
1 **teaspoon salt, or to taste**
1 **tablespoon light soy sauce**
1 **teaspoon sesame oil**
250 **g (8 oz) wonton wrappers peanut oil**

Place the mushrooms in a bowl, add enough hot water to cover. After soaking them for 30 minutes, squeeze out excess moisture, cut off the stems and discard. Chop the mushrooms finely. Peel and devein the prawns, chop them finely. Mix all the chopped ingredients with the minced pork, salt, soy sauce and sesame oil.

Place half a teaspoon of the filling in the centre of each wonton wrapper, moisten the edges of dough with water and fold them to form a triangle with its points slightly overlapping. Press the points together. Bring the two base ends of the triangle together, dabbing with a little filling where they join, and press to seal. When all the wontons are prepared, deep fry a few at a time on medium heat until they are golden. Drain on paper towels. Serve warm.

# pot stickers

*These dumplings are both fried and steamed. Serve with Chinese black vinegar (which is slightly sweet) or diluted malt vinegar mixed with a teaspoon of caster sugar, for dipping.*

makes 30

3 dried shiitake (Chinese) mushrooms
4 to 6 spring onions, finely chopped
250 g (8 oz) minced pork
1 cup finely chopped water chestnuts
1 teaspoon finely grated fresh ginger
1 clove crushed garlic

½ teaspoon salt or to taste
2 teaspoons light soy sauce
1 teaspoon oriental sesame oil
2 teaspoons cornflour
125 ml (4 fl oz) peanut oil, for cooking

**Dough**
2 cups plain flour
250 ml (8 fl oz) boiling water

Soak the mushrooms in hot water for 30 minutes. Discard the stems and chop the caps finely. Mix mushrooms, spring onions, pork, water chestnuts, ginger, garlic, salt, soy sauce and sesame oil. Blend cornflour with 2 tablespoons of cold water and add to mushroom mixture, mixing by hand until thoroughly combined.

Dough: pour boiling water onto the flour in a large bowl, while stirring with chopsticks. When the mixture is combined and cool enough to handle, knead on a lightly floured surface until it is soft and smooth. Form the dough into a cylinder, then roll on a smooth surface until it's a long sausage about 2.5 cm (1 inch) in diameter. Cut roll into 30 equal slices and cover with a damp cloth.

On a lightly floured board, roll out each slice into a circle about 10 cm (4 inches) in diameter. Make overlapping pleats around one side of the circle. Put a teaspoon of filling in the pocket formed by the pleats. Moisten the edges and pinch them together to seal. Cover the dumplings with a damp cloth, keeping them separate so they do not stick together.

Heat a large, heavy-based frying pan over a medium heat and add 4 tablespoons of oil to coat the base and sides. Add half the dumplings, keeping the pleats on top. Cook the dumplings until they are golden underneath, loosening them from the base with a spatula or frying slice to prevent them sticking. Boil 250 ml (8 fl oz) water and 2 tablespoons oil in a separate pan and pour this over the dumplings, loosening any that are inclined to stick. (You can see how they got their name.) Bring the pan to the boil again, covering and cooking the contents for 5 minutes. Lower the heat and cook a further 5 minutes. Uncover the pan and cook the dumplings until the liquid evaporates, lifting dumplings to prevent them sticking. They should be golden and crusty underneath.

Repeat with remaining dumplings. Serve with chilli, soy or sweet vinegar dipping sauce.

# scallops in pastry

makes about 30

250 g (8 oz) scallops
60 g (2 oz) rice vermicelli
1 teaspoon finely grated fresh ginger
½ teaspoon salt
3 teaspoons light soy sauce
2 teaspoons oriental sesame oil
18 snow peas or tender green beans
1 packet (30 sheets) spring roll pastry, 125 mm (5 inch) size
peanut oil for deep-frying

Chop the scallops coarsely. Soak the rice vermicelli in hot water for 10 minutes, then drain it and cut it into 5 cm (2 inch) lengths. Mix it with the ginger, salt, soy and sesame oil. String the snow peas or beans. Blanch the snow peas in boiling water for one minute, the beans for 2 minutes or longer, depending on their tenderness. Drop them into iced water to set their colour. Dry them, slice finely and combine with scallop mixture.

Put a spoonful of filling on a pastry sheet, near one edge. Fold the edge over, then turn in the sides to enclose the filling while continuing to roll. Dampen the edge of the pastry with water to seal it.

Deep fry a few rolls at a time in hot oil. Drain on paper towels when golden brown, and serve warm.

# honey-glazed chicken

*This dish and stuffed chicken wings (see below) are ideal to make together because one requires the top joint of the wing, while the other uses only the middle joint*

serves 6

12 chicken wings, top joint only
60 ml (2 fl oz) dark soy sauce
2 tablespoons honey
1 teaspoon finely grated fresh ginger

Discard the wing tips and divide the wings at the joint. Combine the soy sauce, honey and ginger and marinate the chicken for 20 minutes, turning to coat thoroughly.

Put the chicken into a wok with 125 ml (4 fl oz) water, cover and simmer for 15 minutes or until tender, turning frequently until sauce is thick and coats the pieces with a brown glaze. Serve warm.

# stuffed chicken wings

makes 12

12 chicken wings, middle joint only
½ teaspoon garlic, crushed
½ teaspoon five spice powder
1 tablespoon soy sauce
1 thick slice of ham

1 piece canned winter bamboo shoot
6 Chinese mushrooms, braised in soy sauce, sugar and oil
6 thin spring onions
3 – 4 tablespoons peanut oil for frying

With a small, pointed knife detach the wing bone from the tendon and remove it. Combine the garlic, five spice powder and soy sauce, and rub the chicken with the mixture, inside and out.

Cut the ham, bamboo shoot and braised mushrooms into strips the same length as the chicken joints and push them into the cavity, together with a length of spring onion.

Heat the oil and fry the chicken until it is pale golden. Place the stuffed chicken joints on a heatproof plate and steam them for 10 minutes over boiling water. Serve hot.

# almond -crusted chicken fingers

serves 6

250 g (8 oz) chicken breast fillets
½ teaspoon crushed garlic
½ teaspoon finely grated ginger
½ teaspoon salt
2 teaspoons dry sherry
2 teaspoons cornflour
2 teaspoons egg white
1 cup blanched almonds, chopped
oil for deep-frying

Cut the chicken into fingers and marinate them for 10 minutes in a mixture of the garlic, ginger, salt and sherry. Add the cornflour and egg white, mixing gently. Roll the fingers of chicken in the chopped almonds and firm them into a good shape. Fry the fingers in medium–hot oil, just until the almonds are pale golden. Drain the chicken on paper towels and serve warm with a dipping sauce.

# finger food

# appetisers & finger food

# bhel
## puri

*The proper way to make this wonderfully savoury Indian snack is to prepare a stiff dough, knead it, rest it, roll it extremely thin, cut it into small rounds and deep fry it until crisp. A short cut is to buy a packet of neutral or slightly spicy nibbles. My favourite is soya chips.*

2 cups chips or crisps
2 cups fine sev
3 tablespoons oil
2 cups unsweetened puffed rice
1 teaspoon garam masala (see
    page 91)
½ teaspoon chilli powder
½ teaspoon salt
1 medium onion, finely chopped
2 – 3 fresh green chillies, chopped
1 cup coarsely chopped fresh
    coriander
250 ml (8 fl oz) tamarind chutney
    (see page 89)

If the crisps are large, crush them slightly before adding them to a bowl with the sev. Heat the oil in a wok and quickly fry the puffed rice. Lift the rice out on a slotted spoon, draining it on paper towels while it cools. Mix the garam masala, chilli powder and salt before sprinkling it on the chips, tossing to combine. Combine the chopped onion, chillies and coriander in a small bowl.

Each person quickly combines a serve of the crisp, sprinkled nibbles, the tamarind chutney and the chopped onion mixture, eating it immediately so none of the delightful crunchiness is lost.

# crisp vegetables with shrimp dip

serves 6

⅓ cup dried shrimp
2 small garlic cloves
2 red chillies
3 shallots or 1 medium brown onion
3 teaspoons palm sugar or brown sugar
60 ml (2 fl oz) fish sauce
60 ml (2 fl oz) lime or lemon juice
vegetables in season (choose from radishes, carrots, cucumbers, asparagus, beans)

Soak the shrimp in hot water for 15 minutes, then drain the water off. Remove any sandy tracts. Pound the shrimps to a pulp in a mortar and pestle with the garlic, chillies and shallots. Stir in the sugar, fish sauce, lime juice and 60 ml (2 fl oz) of water. Alternatively, purée the mixture in a blender. Pour into a bowl and arrange vegetables around.

Most of the vegetables may be served raw, but those that need cooking (like beans or asparagus), may be dropped into boiling water for 2 minutes. When tender but still crisp, lift the vegetables out with a slotted spoon and drop them into iced water to preserve their colour and texture. Drain them on paper towels. Cut the remaining vegetables into fancy shapes and crisp them in the refrigerator until required.

To make carrot flowers, cut V-shapes along the length of a carrot, then slice it crossways. To Vandyke a small seedless cucumber, use a sharp, pointed knife to cut a series of evenly spaced points around 8 cm (3 inch) lengths of the cucumber. Then pull the cucumber apart (see photograph on page ii).

# baigan

bartha/eggplant purée

*This dish is usually served as an accompaniment to rice, but it also makes an excellent dip. Roasting the eggplants gives this dish its delicious, smoky flavour.*

serves 6

750 g (1½ lb) large eggplants
3 tablespoons ghee or oil
3 medium onions, finely chopped
2 teaspoons ground coriander
2 teaspoons ground cummin
½ teaspoon chilli powder
2 ripe tomatoes, chopped
¼ cup chopped spring onions
1½ teaspoons salt, or to taste
½ cup chopped fresh coriander
1 teaspoon garam masala (see page 91)

Roast the eggplants over hot coals or a gas flame. Alternatively, place the eggplants under a griller, turning them with tongs until the skin of the vegetable is thoroughly blackened and the flesh soft to touch. After cooling, remove the eggplant's skin and chop the flesh roughly.

Heat the ghee or oil and fry the onions slowly until they are soft and golden brown. Add the ground spices and fry this mixture for one minute. Add the tomatoes, eggplant, spring onions, salt and half the fresh coriander. Cover this mixture and cook it over a low heat until the purée is thick enough to make into a mound with a spoon. Sprinkle the mixture with the remaining fresh coriander and serve it with Indian bread or crisp toast.

# krupuk

*Shrimp wafers come in a variety of shapes, sizes and colours. Those with the best and most distinctive shrimp flavour are the large, roughly oblong, salmon-pink variety. Krupuk are based on a starch and ground shrimp mixture. When deep-fried in oil they become light, crisp and twice their original size.*

500 ml (16 fl oz) peanut oil for deep
frying
12 – 16 large krupuk (or 30 small
ones)
melinjo crackers, optional

Heat the oil in a wok or deep frying pan until a blue haze shimmers over the surface. Test
the oil first. If a small piece of wafer swells within 2–3 seconds of being dropped in, the temperature
is correct. If the wafer sinks to the bottom of the pan and takes time to swell, the krupuk will be tough
and leathery instead of crisp. If the oil is too hot the krupuk will brown too quickly.

Fry the large krupuk one at a time (if your pan is too small, break them in half before
frying). Melinjo crackers can be fried a few at a time. After frying, drain them on absorbent paper and
serve fairly quickly. Cool them thoroughly before storing in an airtight container.

Sometimes, in humid conditions, krupuk absorb moisture and do not puff as they should.
This can be avoided by drying the krupuk in a single layer on a baking tray in a very slow oven.
Cool before frying.

# chilli peanuts

*A hot, crisp accompaniment to serve with pre-dinner drinks.*

2 cups raw peanuts
250 ml (8 fl oz) oil for frying
2 teaspoons garlic, crushed
1 tablespoon sambal oelek, or
finely chopped red chillies
3 tablespoons desiccated coconut
1 teaspoon salt, or to taste

In a wok, fry the peanuts in the oil until they are golden brown. Lift the peanuts out with a slotted spoon and drain them on paper towels.

Pour off all but 2 tablespoons of the oil and, on a low heat, fry the garlic, stirring until it is golden. Add the sambal oelek and fry for one minute more before adding the coconut and salt. Fry a further minute. Return the peanuts to the wok and continue to stir-fry, just until the nuts are well mixed with the sambal oelek or chilli. Serve at room temperature.

# devilled cashews

*Serve as a nibble with drinks. Be warned, however, sit down with a bowl of these nuts and you could demolish the lot yourself.*

serves 20

500 g (1 lb) raw cashews
oil for frying
3 teaspoons salt
2 teaspoons chilli powder

Set aside any broken pieces of cashew as these will burn easily. Heat 750 ml (24 fl oz) of oil in a wok or deep frying pan. Fry one cup of cashews at a time on medium high heat, stirring with a slotted metal spoon. When the cashews are golden, drain them on paper towels. Don't fry the cashews until they are brown because nuts continue to cook in their own heat for a few minutes and may become bitter.

After all the nuts have been fried and drained, transfer them to a sheet of greaseproof paper. Sprinkle them with the combined salt and chilli powder. Toss them well to distribute the seasoning, then allow them to cool completely before storing in an airtight container. They will keep for about a week.

# steamed sago balls

*These translucent, bite-size savouries are suitable for freezing, requiring only a few minutes to steam and serve.*

makes about 50

2 tablespoons peanut oil
1 onion, chopped finely
3 teaspoons pepper and coriander paste (see page 90)
250 g (8 oz) minced pork
2 teaspoons palm sugar or brown sugar
2 tablespoons fish sauce

3 tablespoons crunchy peanut butter
1½ cups sago or pearl tapioca, white or coloured
¼ teaspoon salt
½ cup tapioca flour
1 tablespoon crushed fried shallots or fried garlic flakes

Heat the oil in a wok and fry the onion over a low heat, stirring until soft. Add the pepper and coriander paste and continue to stir and fry until the mixture is fragrant. Add the pork, raise the heat and stir-fry until the pork is browned. Add the sugar and the fish sauce, stirring to distribute the flavours. Cover and cook this mixture on a low heat until the mixture is almost dry. Remove it from the heat and mix in the peanut butter before cooling.

Rinse the sago in a fine sieve, draining away any excess water. Transfer the sago into a bowl and gradually mix in 60 ml (2 fl oz) salted hot water. Mix this well before covering and leaving for one hour. Take heaped teaspoonsful of sago with a wet spoon and roll them into balls in dampened palms. Cover the balls with a damp cloth. Wash and dry the hands well and dust them with tapioca flour. Make an indentation in each ball to form a cup. Into this cup place a small teaspoon of filling. Seal the sago over the filling, moulding the filled sago into balls once more. Cover them with a damp cloth.

Place oiled paper strips in a steamer and arrange the balls on them, leaving a little space for swelling. Steam the balls on the paper strips over the boiling water for 15–20 minutes, or until the sago is clear. Remove the steamer from the heat and leave it for 5 minutes before placing balls on a serving dish. Garnish with crushed, fried shallots or a pinch of crushed, fried garlic. For a less pungent garnish, use crushed roasted peanuts or chopped coriander. Serve hot or at room temperature.

**Note** The steamed sago balls are shown on page 31 with the steamed pork and crab moulds.

# steamed
## pork and crab moulds

makes about 20

125 g (4 oz) pork mince
125 g (4 oz) chicken mince
125 g (4 oz) crab meat, cooked
2 teaspoons pepper and coriander paste (see page 90)
2 tablespoons spring onion, finely chopped
1 tablespoon fish sauce

2 tablespoons canned coconut milk
1 teaspoon palm sugar or brown sugar
1 egg
1 red chilli, sliced finely
few coriander or basil leaves

Combine the minced pork, chicken and crab meat, discarding any bony bits.

Add the pepper and coriander paste, spring onion, fish sauce, coconut milk and sugar, mixing them all together thoroughly. Press the mixture into small greased cups, about the size of Chinese wine cups.

Separate the egg and beat each part slightly. Put the yolk on some of the cups,

and the white on others. Steam the filled cups over boiling water for 20 minutes. Cool them and remove the moulds from the cups, garnishing with a slice of chilli or a leaf of coriander or basil.

# lumpia

*This Philippine version of spring rolls may be served fried or fresh. The fried version are wrapped in spring roll pastry. For fresh lumpia, the filling is enclosed first in a lettuce leaf and then in Asian rice paper; not the western kind used in baking.*

makes 12–16

2 tablespoons oil
1 tablespoon annatto seeds, optional
2 teaspoons finely chopped garlic
1 cup green beans, sliced diagonally
2 cups cooked and diced chicken
1 cup cooked pork in fine strips
1 cup small cooked prawns, shelled
1 cup finely diced water chestnuts
2 cups finely sliced Chinese cabbage (wongah bak)
½ cup finely sliced spring onions
1 tablespoon light soy sauce
salt and pepper to taste
12 – 16 cos lettuce leaves
12 – 16 round rice paper sheets

Heat the oil and fry the annatto seeds over a low heat, stirring, until the oil is bright orange in colour. Remove the seeds with a slotted spoon and discard them. Cook the garlic gently for a few seconds in the coloured and flavoured oil, then add the sliced beans and stir-fry them for 3 minutes or until they are tender but still crisp. Allow the beans to cool. Add the meat, vegetables (excluding lettuce), sauce and seasonings and toss well.

Dip a sheet of rice paper into lukewarm water for a few seconds to make it pliable. Place it on the work surface. Lay a cos lettuce leaf on the rice paper and add a portion of the cooled filling. Roll it up so that one end is enclosed, with leaf showing at other end. Serve accompanied by sweet-sour sauce (see page 88) with a dash of soy sauce stirred in.

# fish koftas

500 g (1 lb) canned fish
500 g (1 lb) potatoes
1 cup finely chopped onion
1 egg, beaten
1 cup soft breadcrumbs
1½ teaspoons salt
½ teaspoon ground black pepper
1 teaspoon ground coriander

½ teaspoon ground cummin
1 tablespoon finely chopped fresh dill
1 tablespoon finely chopped fresh chilli
dry breadcrumbs or cornflake crumbs
oil for deep-frying

Drain the fish thoroughly, pressing out the liquid. Boil the potatoes and mash them while they are hot. Combine the fish, potatoes, onion, egg, fresh breadcrumbs, salt, spices, dill and chillies, mixing them thoroughly. Shape the mixture into 60 small balls and roll them in the dry crumbs.

Heat the oil and deep-fry a few balls at a time, over a medium heat (if the oil is too hot the coating will not stay on the balls). Lift the golden brown balls out with a slotted spoon and drain them on paper towels.

# deep-fried calamari balls

makes 30 to 40

2½ cups finely diced bread
500 g (1 lb) squid or cuttlefish tubes
1 teaspoon salt
1 teaspoon sugar
1 teaspoon oriental sesame oil
750 ml (24 fl oz) oil for deep-frying

Trim the crusts off several slices of stale bread. Cut the slices into 4 mm (⅛ inch) strips, then dice into tiny squares. Spread them on a large sheet of paper.

Wash the squid or cuttlefish, cleaning out any sand inside the tube. Chop the tube finely with a sharp knife or in a food processor and mix the pieces with salt, sugar and sesame oil. With oiled palms roll teaspoonsful of the mixture into 2 cm (¾ inch) balls. Roll these in the diced bread until they are covered completely.

Heat the frying oil and deep-fry a few at a time until they are golden. Do not overcook the squid or it will toughen. Drain the balls on paper towels and serve warm. Offer sweet chilli sauce or sweet-sour sauce (see page 88) for dipping.

# samosas

makes 30 or 40

1 quantity savoury mince filling made with lamb
10 sheets spring roll pastry, 25 cm (10 inch) size
oil for deep-frying

**Savoury Mince Filling**
1 tablespoon oil
2 medium onions, chopped finely
1 teaspoon finely chopped garlic
1 teaspoon finely chopped fresh ginger

3 teaspoons curry powder
½ teaspoon salt
1 tablespoon lemon juice
250 g (8 oz) minced beef or lamb
1 medium potato, peeled and diced small
1 teaspoon garam masala (see page 91)
¼ cup chopped fresh mint or coriander

Prepare the savoury mince filling. Heat the oil and gently fry the onions, garlic and ginger until they are golden. Add the curry powder, salt and lemon juice and fry again briefly. Add the meat and stir-fry until it is brown. Stir in 250 ml (8 fl oz) of hot water, cover and simmer for 10 minutes. Add the potato and cook until it is soft and the liquid is absorbed. Stir in the garam masala and herbs. Cool.

Cut the sheets of spring roll pastry into 3 or 4 equal strips. Separate the sheets but cover with plastic or a slightly damp tea towel to prevent them drying out. Taking one strip at a time, put a spoonful of filling at one end and fold the pastry over diagonally. Fold it again and again, keeping the edges lined up so the filling is enclosed in a perfect triangle. Moisten the end of the strip with water and press it lightly to seal.

When all the samosas are made, heat about 750 ml (24 fl oz) of oil in a wok or deep frying pan and fry a few at a time until golden. Drain them on a paper towels and serve warm or at room temperature, with a mint or coriander dip with yoghurt (see page 89).

# prawn
## pastries

makes 30

500 g (1 lb) raw prawns, shelled and
deveined
2 tablespoons ghee or oil
2 onions, finely chopped
1 teaspoon each finely chopped
garlic and ginger
1 teaspoon ground turmeric
½ teaspoon chilli powder
1 teaspoon salt or to taste
ready-rolled shortcrust pastry

Chop the prawns coarsely. Heat the ghee or oil and cook the onions, garlic and ginger gently until they are soft and golden. Add the spices and fry a minute longer, then add the prawns and fry until they are cooked.

Season to taste and cool the mixture before enclosing a teaspoonful in a circle or square of pastry. Dampen the edges and press it to seal. Bake the pastries in a moderately hot oven until they are golden. Serve warm.

# Thai
prawn balls

makes 20

250 g (8 oz) raw prawn meat,
     deveined
2 teaspoons pepper and coriander
     paste (see page 90)
2 teaspoons fish sauce
1 cup spring onions, finely
     chopped
1 cup roasted rice powder or
     dried breadcrumbs
oil for frying

Chop the prawns finely and mix them with pepper and coriander paste, fish sauce and

spring onions. Form the mixture into small balls, dipping each into rice powder or breadcrumbs before

frying in the hot oil until golden brown.

# devilled prawns

serves 12

750 g (1½ lb) raw prawns, medium size
2 tablespoons oil
1½ cups finely chopped onion
2 teaspoons finely chopped garlic
1 teaspoon salt
1 teaspoon chilli powder
2 teaspoons paprika
¼ teaspoon turmeric
1 tablespoon fish sauce
1 tablespoon tomato paste
2 teaspoons sugar

Shell and devein prawns. Heat oil and gently cook onions and garlic, stirring frequently, until translucent and golden. Add salt and spices and fry for a minute or two longer, then add prawns, fish sauce and ¼ cup water. Cover and simmer for 10 minutes. Stir in tomato paste and sugar and cook uncovered for a few minutes until sauce is thick enough to coat prawns. Serve with wooden cocktail sticks pushed into each prawn, or place prawns on bite-size fried croutons.

# Dutch meatballs

makes about 40

30 g (1 oz) butter
1 cup finely chopped onion
500 g (1 lb) minced steak
½ cup soft white breadcrumbs
1½ teaspoons salt
½ teaspoon ground black pepper
2 teaspoons chopped fresh dill
¼ teaspoon ground cinnamon

¼ teaspoon ground cloves
1 teaspoon crushed garlic
½ teaspoon finely grated fresh
  ginger
squeeze of lemon juice
1 egg, beaten
dry breadcrumbs for coating
oil for frying

Heat the butter in a small frying pan and gently fry the onion until it is soft. Combine the onion with the minced steak, breadcrumbs, salt and pepper, dill, cinnamon, cloves, garlic, ginger and lemon juice. Mix the ingredients thoroughly and form them into small balls (about 2.5 cm [1 inch] in diameter). Dip the balls into the beaten egg and coat them with dry breadcrumbs. Deep-fry the balls in hot oil until they are golden brown. Drain them on paper towels before serving.

# savoury vegetable fritters

*This batter has been lightened with self-raising flour to lessen the strong chickpea flavour.*

**makes about 36**

½ cup chickpea flour (besan)
1 cup self-raising flour
1 teaspoon garam masala
  salt to taste
½ teaspoon ground turmeric
1 teaspoon garlic, crushed
4 cups raw vegetables of choice,
  cut into small dice or thin
  slices — suggest eggplant,
  zucchini, onion, potato,
  pumpkin, cauliflower,
  capsicum, spinach leaves

Sieve the chickpea flour, self-raising flour, garam masala, salt and turmeric into bowl. Add 250 ml (8 fl oz) of water, stirring to make a thick batter. Add the garlic and mix it in well. Rest the batter for 30 minutes, but beat it again before adding the vegetables.

Stir the vegetables into the batter then drop teaspoonsful of the mixture into the deep, hot oil. Fry just a few at a time so the oil stays hot, ensuring tender, light fritters. Drain the golden brown fritters on paper towels.

A second frying is the secret to crispness. Just before serving, reheat the oil until it is very hot. Repeat the frying process, cooking each batch for only 30 seconds before draining on paper towels. Serve warm with tamarind chutney (see page 89).

# stuffed eggs

makes 12

6 eggs
½ – 1 teaspoon chilli bean paste
2 teaspoons sweet chilli sauce,
   strained
3 tablespoons mayonnaise
   salt to taste
   chilli slices and coriander sprigs

Place the eggs in cold water and bring them to the boil over a gentle heat. Simmer the eggs for 10 minutes, stirring gently for the first 3 or 4 minutes to centre the yolks. Cool the eggs quickly in a bowl of iced water, then shell and cut them into halves. Scoop the yolks into a bowl and mash them, adding the chilli bean paste, chilli sauce, mayonnaise and salt. Pipe or spoon this mixture into the egg whites, garnishing with chilli and coriander, before chilling for one hour.

# quail egg flowers

makes 12

1 dozen fresh quail eggs (canned
   are not suitable)
1 tablespoon nam prik pao (see
   page 91)
6 small cucumbers
  few chives

Hard boil the quail eggs for 8 minutes. Cool and shell the eggs, cutting a slice off the rounded end of each egg. Scoop out the yolks and mix with them with nam prik pao. Replace this mixture in the white of the egg. Place each egg in a cup hollowed from the end of a small cucumber. Secure the egg with a cocktail stick threaded through a length of chive.

**Note** The quail eggs can be coloured with a paste of turmeric and paprika and a little water, left on for 30 minutes before rinsing off.

# galloping horses

*This delicious dish consists of a savoury pork and peanut mixture, placed on top fresh fruit.*

makes about 30

375 g (12 oz) minced pork
2 tablespoons oil
2 teaspoons garlic, finely chopped
2 teaspoons finely chopped coriander roots
3 tablespoons crushed roasted peanuts
2 fresh red chillies, seeded

2 tablespoons fish sauce
¼ teaspoon black pepper
3 tablespoons palm or brown sugar
oil for frying
mandarin segments or fresh pineapple slices
coriander leaves

Place the pork mince in a bowl. Heat the oil and fry the garlic and coriander roots over a low heat until they are soft and golden. Add this to the pork, then add the peanuts and one finely-chopped chilli, the fish sauce, pepper and sugar. Mix these well. Form the mixture into about 30 small balls, flattening each ball slightly. Pour just enough oil into a heavy frying pan to cover the base. Fry the pork patties over a medium–low heat until they are well browned on one side, then fry the other side. Drain the patties on paper towel and allow them to cool.

Remove all traces of pith from the mandarin segments but leave the fine membrane. Cut each segment open down its back and place the resulting circles on a serving dish. If pineapple is used, cut it into thin, bite-sized pieces. Place the pork patties on the fruit and garnish them with small pieces of sliced chilli and coriander leaves.

# chicken toast

makes 24

250 g (8 oz) chicken fillets
1 rasher fatty bacon
2 tablespoons water chestnuts or celery, finely chopped
2 tablespoons spring onions, finely chopped
½ teaspoon finely grated ginger
½ teaspoon crushed garlic

1 tablespoon cornflour
1 tablespoon oyster sauce
½ teaspoon oriental sesame oil
12 slices white sandwich bread, crusts removed
½ cup toasted sesame seeds
750 ml (24 fl oz) peanut oil

Dice the chicken and bacon and mince them in the food processor. In a bowl mix the minced chicken with the rest of the ingredients except the bread, sesame seeds and peanut oil. Combine these ingredients thoroughly and spread on slices of bread. Cut the bread into triangles or fingers and dip these in sesame seeds, pressing the seeds on firmly.

Heat the peanut oil in a wok or deep frying pan and deep-fry a few pieces of the coated bread at a time, chicken side downwards. Remove the pieces when they are golden brown and drain them on paper towels. Serve warm or at room temperature.

# Thai fish cakes

makes 12

250 g (8 oz) fillets bream or other
    white fish
2 teaspoons red curry paste (see
    below)
2 teaspoons fish sauce
½ teaspoon finely grated lime rind
    pinch of white pepper
125 ml (4 fl oz) canned coconut milk

1 tablespoon finely chopped
    spring onions or chives
2 teaspoons rice flour
¼ teaspoon salt
    red chillies, seeded and sliced
    fine shreds of fresh kaffir lime
    leaves
    small basil leaves, optional

Preheat the oven to hot, 200°C (400°F). Prepare the fish by removing the skin and any bones and dice the fillets. Finely chop them in a food processor. Add the curry paste, fish sauce, lime rind, pepper and 2 tablespoons of the coconut milk. Process this mixture to a paste. Turn the mixture into a bowl and mix in spring onions or chives so the mixture is speckled with green. Divide it into 12 portions of equal size and, with oiled palms, roll each into a ball. Press the balls into oiled patty pans to flatten them. Bake the patties for 5 or 6 minutes, or steam them over boiling water for 8 to 10 minutes.

Combine in a saucepan the remaining coconut milk, rice flour and salt. Stir it over a low heat until it has thickened. Spoon a little of this onto each fish cake. Decorate the cakes with a chilli slice, shreds of lime leaf and a small basil leaf.

# red curry paste

makes 1 cup

6 fresh hot chillies
2 small brown onions
1 teaspoon each black peppercorns,
    turmeric, shrimp paste and salt
2 teaspoons each paprika, ground
    cummin and ground coriander

1 tablespoon each finely chopped garlic,
    lemon grass and galangal in brine
2 tablespoons chopped fresh coriander
    roots

Roughly chop the chillies and put into an electric blender with all the other ingredients. Blend to a smooth paste, adding a little water if necessary to facilitate blending. Store in a glass jar in the refrigerator and always use a clean, dry spoon to measure amount needed.

# deep-fried prawn toast

*For a more economical version, halve the quantity of prawns and use an equal amount of boneless white fish fillets. Process to a smooth paste together with the other ingredients.*

makes 48 pieces

12 slices stale white or wholemeal
 bread (not wholegrain)
500 g (1 lb) uncooked prawns
1 egg white
60 g (2 oz) pork or bacon fat
1 spring onion, white portion only
2 teaspoons oriental sesame oil
½ teaspoon sugar

½ teaspoon salt, or to taste
¼ teaspoon white pepper
 oil for deep-frying

Trim the crusts off the bread and spread it on a tray to dry slightly. Shell and devein the prawns. If using a food processor, process the prawns with the egg white, pork fat and roughly chopped spring onion. Add the sesame oil and seasonings, processing until they are combined.

If the mixture is to be minced by hand, use a large chef's knife or cleaver. Finely mince the spring onion, add the pork fat and chop it until minced. Finely chop the prawns and mix them thoroughly with the other ingredients.

Spread the bread slices with the prawn mixture and cut each slice into quarters. In a wok or frying pan, heat the oil and fry the bread, prawn side down, a few pieces at a time. When golden, lift out the toast pieces and drain them on paper towels. Serve warm.

**Note** Photograph of deep-fried prawn toast is on page 51 with the Thai fish cakes

# picnic & lunchbox

# satays with peanut sauce

*In Asia, satays are served with cakes of pressed rice, but they taste just as wonderful on a crusty roll.*

serves 6

750 g (1½ lb) beef or pork fillet
1 large onion, chopped roughly
2 strips lemon rind
2 tablespoons light soy sauce
3 teaspoons ground coriander
1½ teaspoons ground cummin

1 teaspoon ground turmeric
1 teaspoon salt or to taste
1 teaspoon palm sugar or brown sugar
¼ cup roasted peanuts

Cut meat into small cubes, no larger than 2 cm (¾ inch). Put remaining ingredients into blender or food processor and blend to a purée. Pour over meat, mix well so all pieces are coated with marinade, cover and leave for 1 hour. Soak bamboo skewers in cold water while meat marinates.

Thread 5 or 6 pieces on skewer to cover about half the skewer. Grill over barbecue until meat is browned and cooked through. Serve with crunchy peanut sauce (see page 90).

# minced lamb patties, picnic-style

serves 6

750 g (1½ lb) minced lamb
1 cup finely chopped onion
1½ teaspoons crushed garlic
1 teaspoon salt or to taste
1 teaspoon garam masala

2 teaspoons finely grated fresh ginger
¼ cup finely chopped fresh coriander leaves
1 teaspoon sugar
1 tablespoon sultanas, chopped

In a bowl combine lamb, onion, garlic crushed to a smooth purée with salt, and garam masala. Mix well with hands to evenly distribute seasonings and divide into 6 equal portions. Combine ginger, coriander, sugar and sultanas and divide into 6. With thumb, make a hollow in lamb and put a portion of ginger mixture inside, then shape into a patty.

Cook on a hot griddle or over barbecue grill and serve with flat bread or slipped into bread rolls or hamburger buns. Serve with a crisp salad of diced radish and cucumber in yoghurt dressing.

# pancake rolls

makes 12 to 14

1 quantity savoury mince filling
(see samosas, page 38), made
with beef
1 cup spring onions, finely
chopped
2 fresh chillies, seeded and
chopped
2 tablespoons chopped fresh dill,
optional
2 eggs, beaten
dry breadcrumbs for coating
peanut oil for shallow-frying

**Basic crepe batter**
3 eggs
1¼ cups plain flour
125 ml (4 fl oz) milk
125 ml (4 fl oz) water
pinch salt

Prepare the basic crepe batter. Beat the eggs, mix in the milk and water, then add the flour and salt sifted together. Beat this until it is smooth. Strain the batter into a bowl, cover and leave it to rest for one hour while the filling is prepared.

Add chopped spring onions, chillies and dill to the beef filling after it has been cooked and cooled. Cook thin crepes on a lightly-greased, heavy crepe or omelette pan, cooking until golden on the underside and just set on top. Pile the cooked crepes on a plate.

Put 2 tablespoons of filling on the darker side of each crepe, rolling the pancake up to enclose the filling, tucking in the sides as you go. Brush the edge with beaten egg to seal it. When all the crepes are made, dip each one in the beaten egg and then in the breadcrumbs, pressing them on firmly. Shallow-fry in hot oil just deep enough to cover base of heavy frying pan, turning the rolls with tongs until the crumbs are golden brown and crisp.

# rice
## paper rolls

*Rice paper rolls may be fresh or fried. The fresh rolls are lower in calories.*

makes 16 to 18

1 cup dried shrimp
½ cup rice vermicelli
2 tablespoons shredded dried
   radish
1 tablespoon bottled ginger
   shreds
2 red chillies, sliced
1 tablespoon fish sauce

2 tablespoons lime or lemon juice
2 teaspoons sugar
16 – 18 rice paper sheets
250 g (8 oz) small cooked prawns,
   shelled and deveined
   fresh basil leaves
   lettuce leaves

Soak the dried shrimp in hot water for 10 minutes, then drain and chop it or shred it in a food processor. Soak the rice vermicelli in very hot water for 10 minutes, then drain it in a colander. Cut it into short lengths. Simmer the shredded radish in a little water for 5 minutes, drain, then mix it with the shrimp, noodles, ginger and chillies. Dissolve the sugar in the fish sauce and lime juice, pour it over the mixture and toss well.

Put warm water into a shallow dish wide enough for the sheets of rice paper. Dip each sheet briefly (5 seconds) and place it on a flat surface. Place 2 or 3 prawns on the paper, adding a heaped tablespoon of rice vermicelli filling, and basil leaves rolled tightly in a piece of lettuce. Bring the ends of the paper together and roll up firmly, enclosing the filling. Arrange on a platter and keep covered with a slightly damp cloth until served.

# Malaysian curry pies

makes 14 to 16
small pies

**Sweet-salt pastry**
2 cups plain flour
1½ tablespoons custard powder
1 teaspoon salt
2 tablespoons caster sugar
90 g (3 oz) cold lard
90 g (3 oz) cold butter
beaten egg to glaze

250g (½ lb) chicken thigh fillets
1 medium potato
1 large onion, chopped finely
1 teaspoon finely chopped garlic

1 teaspoon finely chopped fresh ginger
1 teaspoon finely chopped galangal
1 tablespoon ground coriander
2 teaspoons ground cummin
½ teaspoon ground turmeric
¼ teaspoon ground fennel
250 ml (8 fl oz) canned coconut milk
1 stem lemon grass or 3 strips lemon rind
1 teaspoon palm sugar or brown sugar
1 teaspoon salt

Prepare the pastry by sifting the flour and custard powder into a bowl, and stirring in the salt and sugar. Rub in the lard. Cut the butter in 2.5 cm (1 inch) pieces and toss it through the mixture. Add 5 or 6 tablespoons of iced water and knead the mixture lightly into a soft dough. On a floured board roll the dough into a rectangle 45 x 20 cm (18 x 8 inches). Fold this into thirds, turning so the open ends are at the top and bottom. Roll and fold the dough again. If the dough becomes too soft, wrap it in plastic and chill till firm. Roll and fold a third time, then leave the dough to rest for 30 minutes in the refrigerator.

Trim any excess fat off the chicken and cut it into small pieces. Peel and dice the potatoes. In a saucepan or wok, combine the onions, garlic, ginger, galangal, ground spices and coconut milk with 125 ml (4 fl oz) of water. Stir this mixture over a medium heat until it comes to the boil. Add the lemon grass or rind and simmer the mixture gently for 5 minutes. Add the chicken and potatoes, continuing to simmer until they are tender. Stir in the sugar and salt and cook the mixture until the liquid is almost completely reduced. After cooling, remove the lemon grass or rind. Mash some of the potato into the gravy to make it very thick.

Roll the pastry on a floured surface to 6 mm (¼ inch) thickness. Cut twelve 7.5 cm (3 inch) circles to line the base of pie moulds. Cut slightly smaller circles for the tops. Fill the lined moulds with a tablespoon of chicken mixture, then brush the edges with water and press on the pastry lids. Glaze the lids with beaten egg and bake the pies in a preheated hot oven, 210°C (425°F), for 20 minutes or until golden.

# Thai curry puffs

makes about 36

**Thai mince curry**
2 tablespoons oil
2 tablespoons pepper and
   coriander paste (see page 90)
2 teaspoons ground coriander
1 teaspoon ground turmeric
1 teaspoon ground cummin
750 g (1½ lb) minced beef or pork
3 tablespoons fish sauce
1 cup finely diced raw potato
3 teaspoons sugar
1 hot chilli, chopped finely

**Curry puff pastry**
2 cups plain (all purpose) flour
½ teaspoon salt
60 g (2 oz) butter
60 ml (2 fl oz) canned coconut milk

oil for deep-frying

Prepare the mince curry by heating the oil in a wok or saucepan and frying the pepper and coriander paste and ground spices over a gentle heat, stirring frequently, until fragrant. Add the beef or pork and stir-fry on medium high heat until it browns. Add the fish sauce and simmer, covered, for about 20 minutes. Stir in the potato and sugar, cover and simmer for a further 10 minutes or until the potato is cooked but firm and all the liquid is absorbed. Stir in the chilli and allow it to cool.

Prepare the pastry by sifting the flour and salt, rubbing in the butter and adding sufficient coconut milk to make a fairly firm dough. Knead the dough lightly, form it into a ball and chill, wrapped in plastic film for at least 30 minutes. Roll out the pastry to no more than 3 mm (⅛ inch) thickness and cut it into 10 cm (4 inch) circles with a scone cutter. Brush the edges with cold water, placing a spoonful of filling in the centre and folding the pastry over, pressing it to make a seal. Mark the edges with a fork, or fold to make a rope edge (fold one corner over at a 45 degree angle and press it flat. Fold the next section over to make a triangle over the first fold. Continue in this way, pressing each fold as you go).

Heat the oil and deep-fry a few pastries at a time until they are golden brown. Make sure the oil is hot enough to reach the required colour in 2 minutes. If the oil is not hot enough the pastry will be greasy and heavy. Drain the pastries on paper towels.

# Indian
## curry puffs

makes about 36

**Pastry**
3 cups plain flour
1 teaspoon salt
1 tablespoon soft butter or ghee
   approximately 1 cup lukewarm
   water

**Filling**
1 tablespoon oil or ghee
1 clove garlic, finely chopped
½ teaspoon finely chopped fresh
   ginger

2 medium onions, finely chopped
3 teaspoons mild curry powder
   salt to taste
1 tablespoon lime or lemon juice
375 g (12 oz) minced lamb or beef
1 medium potato, peeled and
   diced
1 teaspoon garam masala
2 tablespoons chopped fresh mint
   oil for deep frying

Pastry: Sift the flour with the salt, rub in the butter and add 250 ml (8 fl oz) of lukewarm water. Mix this well to form soft dough. Knead the dough for 10 minutes until it is smooth and elastic. Wrap the dough in plastic and leave it to rest while preparing the filling.

Filling: Heat the oil in a wok or saucepan. Fry the garlic, ginger and onion, stirring, until the onion softens. Stir in the curry powder, salt and lime juice. Add the minced meat and cook the mixture on a high heat, stirring, until the meat changes colour. Add the potatoes and 125 ml (4 fl oz) of hot water. Stir the mixture well and cover, simmering until the meat and potatoes are tender and all the liquid is absorbed, stirring from time to time towards the end of cooking. Sprinkle on garam masala and chopped mint and leave the meat mixture to cool.

Shape the dough into small balls and roll them out on a lightly floured surface into 20 cm (8 inch) rounds. Cut each round in thirds. Place a tablespoon of filling on one side of a part-circle, then brush around the edges with water. Fold the pastry over to enclose the mixture and press the edges together firmly to form a triangle. When all the pastries are prepared, heat the oil and deep-fry a few at a time until they are golden brown all over. Drain them on paper towels.

# chicken croquettes

makes 20 to 22

250 g (8 oz) chicken thigh fillets
1 tablespoon butter or oil
½ cup sliced shallots or spring
   onions
½ cup finely diced carrots
½ cup sliced green beans
1 teaspoon chopped green chilli
1 teaspoon salt or to taste
¼ teaspoon white pepper
1 teaspoon chicken stock powder
   or crumbled stock cube

500 ml (16 fl oz) thick white sauce
2 tablespoons chopped fresh
   coriander
   dry breadcrumbs for coating
3 tablespoons sesame seeds,
   optional
3 eggs, beaten
   oil for frying

Cut the chicken into small pieces, discarding any pockets of fat. Heat the butter or oil and, on a low heat, cook the shallots and carrots for 5 minutes. Stir in the chicken and cook it until it is no longer pink. Add the beans and chilli and cook the mixture until the liquid evaporates. Season the tender chicken and vegetables with salt, pepper and chicken stock powder.

Mix in the white sauce and coriander, then refrigerate the mixture until it is cold and firm before shaping spoonfuls into croquettes. Dip each croquette into the mixed breadcrumbs and sesame seeds. Press them on firmly. Dip each croquette into the egg again and re-coat it with the breadcrumb mixture. Leave the croquettes to dry for 30 minutes before frying them in hot oil for 2 minutes, until just golden. Drain them on paper towels.

**Note** For a thick white sauce, melt 60 g (2 oz) butter in a heavy-based saucepan and gently cook 4 tablespoons plain flour, stirring, for a few minutes. The flour should not brown. Whisk in 500 ml (16 fl oz) of milk and stir or whisk constantly until it boils and thickens and is perfectly smooth. Cool.

# split
## pea croquettes (masala vadai)

*In those countries where meat is eaten only occasionally or not at all, the main source of protein is pulses and lentils. Apart from the ever-present dhal or lentil purée served with rice, there are numerous snacks based on either whole or split lentils, or lentil flour. Here is a favourite which has many variations.*

**makes about 25 to 30**

- 2 cups yellow split peas
- 1 tablespoon pounded Maldive fish pieces, optional
- 2 tablespoons finely sliced golden shallots
- ½ teaspoon turmeric
- ½ teaspoon chilli powder, or to taste
- 3 sprigs tender curry leaves
- 1½ teaspoons salt, or to taste
- 2 fresh green chillies, sliced few whole school prawns in shell, optional oil for deep-frying

Wash the split peas well and soak overnight or for at least 4 hours. Drain them well. Set aside a quarter of the peas (they will be used whole to give extra crunch) and put remainder into a food processor with all ingredients except prawns and oil. Process until peas are ground finely.

Turn into a bowl, mix in reserved split peas, form into walnut-size balls and flatten slightly. If using prawns, press a prawn onto one side of each croquette. Heat at least 3 cups of oil in a wok or deep frying pan and keep oil at moderate temperature. If too hot they will brown outside and not be cooked through.

Fry no more than 4 or 5 at a time, spooning hot oil over and turning to brown evenly. Drain on paper towels. Taste one or two after the first batch has been fried to make sure mixture is cooked through and to check seasoning. More salt or chilli may be added if preferred. Serve warm or at room temperature.

# potato
## and meat croquettes

makes 16 to 20

1 **quantity savoury mince filling (see samosas, page 38), made with beef**
1 **kg (2 lb) potatoes**
  **salt and pepper to taste**
2 **eggs, beaten**
  **dry breadcrumbs for coating**
  **peanut oil for deep-frying**

Prepare the savoury mince and, if preferred, add the spring onions, chillies and dill as for pancake rolls (see page 56).

Boil the potatoes until tender, drain, peel and mash smoothly, seasoning to taste with salt and pepper. Take 2 tablespoons of the mashed potato in one hand and flatten it, placing a tablespoon of savoury mince in the centre. Mould the potato around the mince in an oval shape. Mould the remaining potato and meat similarly. Dip the croquettes in beaten egg, then in breadcrumbs. These may be refrigerated until required.

Heat the oil in a wok or a deep frying pan and slip in 3 or 4 croquettes at a time. Keep turning them or gently splashing oil over them so they cook to an even, deep golden brown. Drain them on paper towels.

# beef
### and coconut patties

*These Indonesian-style patties make great fillings for pocket bread. Try adding crisp shredded lettuce, sliced radishes, raw onion rings and tomato slices.*

**makes 20 to 22**

375 g (12 oz) minced beef
1 teaspoon dried shrimp paste
2 teaspoons garlic, crushed
2 teaspoons kachai in brine or
   ½ teaspoon ground kencur
1 teaspoon salt
½ teaspoon ground black pepper
2 teaspoons ground coriander
1 teaspoon ground cummin
1 large egg, beaten
1 cup fresh grated or desiccated
   coconut
   oil for frying

Put the beef into a large bowl. Wrap the shrimp paste in foil, press to flatten it and roast it for about 2 minutes on each side under a hot griller. Dissolve this in a little hot water. Add it with the garlic, galangal, salt, pepper and ground spices to the beaten egg and mix well. Pour this mixture over the meat and mix well. Toss the coconut with 4 tablespoons water to moisten, add it to the meat mixture and mix it thoroughly with the hands. Form small patties and shallow-fry them until they are crisp and golden brown. Drain them on paper towels.

**Note** For those who eschew red meat, these tasty patties may be adapted using minced chicken or finely chopped tuna. I might also mention, for those who have a sensitivity to certain preservatives, that fresh grated coconut will be preferable to desiccated coconut. The latter has sulphur dioxide added, and the maximum permitted level is 50 mg per kg. The good news is that grated coconut is increasingly available in Asian stores, either fresh or frozen without additives, but always check the labels first.

sweets

# steamed rice moulds

*Known as lansong in the Philippines, these chewy little moulds are typical of the snacks made in many Asian countries.*

makes about 25

1 cup white glutinous rice
²/₃ cup sugar
125 ml (4 fl oz) canned coconut milk
2 tablespoons cooked rice
3 teaspoons baking powder
food colouring, optional
freshly grated coconut

Soak the glutinous rice in 250 ml (8 fl oz) of water overnight. In the morning, put it in a blender with the sugar, coconut milk, cooked rice and baking powder. Cover and blend on a high speed until the mixture is smooth, colouring with food colours, if preferred.

Pour the mixture into small cups such as Chinese wine cups, each containing only about a tablespoon or two. Place these on the rack of a steamer and steam them over fast-boiling water for 25 minutes. Remove the steamer from the heat and let the cakes stand in the steamer to cool gradually for 10 minutes. Uncover the steamer and allow the cakes to cool completely.

Gently loosen the cakes from the sides of the cups with a small spatula or table knife. If they are difficult to remove, run a few drops of cold water into the cup around the rice cake. Turn them out and roll in grated coconut.

# oriental melon with sweet wontons

1 **watermelon or honeydew**
**melon**
1 **can longans**
1 **can mandarin segments**

Wash and dry the melon, cut off the top third and scallop the edges. With a melon baller

scoop out the flesh, discarding the seeds. Put the melon balls into a bowl with longans and mandarins

and some syrup from the cans. Cover and chill. Fill the shell with fruits just before serving. Sweet

wontons may be served alongside.

# sweet wontons

1½ **cups stoned dates, chopped**
½ **cup walnut kernels, finely**
   **chopped**
1 **teaspoon orange or lemon rind,**
   **finely grated**
   **squeeze of orange juice**

1 **packet wonton pastry**
   **(60 squares)**
   **peanut oil for deep-frying**
   **icing sugar for dusting**

Mix the dates with chopped nuts, grated rind and enough juice to moisten the mixture.

Form the mixture into small cylinders, placing one diagonally on each square of wonton pastry and

rolling it up so the filling is completely enclosed. Twist the ends of the pastry to make a seal. Fry a

few at a time in deep, hot oil until they are golden brown. Remove with a slotted spoon and drain on

paper towels. Sprinkle with icing sugar.

# peach buns

makes 16

30 g (1 oz) compressed yeast or
    2 teaspoons active dry yeast
1 teaspoon sugar
250 ml (8 fl oz) water
2½ cups self-raising flour
½ cup plain flour
2 tablespoons caster sugar
1 tablespoon lard
1 cup sweet lotus nut paste or
    sweetened black bean paste
red food colouring

Make the dough by combining the yeast, sugar and warm water in a bowl, stirring and leaving it in a warm place until frothy. Put both flours and the caster sugar into a bowl and rub in the lard. Add the yeast mixture and stir it, turning the dough onto a floured surface. Knead it for 10 minutes, then leave it covered in a warm place to rise. After it has proved the first time, punch it down and divide it into 16 equal portions. Roll each into a smooth ball, and cover with a damp cloth while filling and shaping buns.

Make a hollow in each ball of dough to fill with teaspoonsful of lotus nut paste rolled into balls. Mould the dough around the paste balls. Shape the dough like a peach, pulling out a small point of dough at one end and making a crease on one side with the back of a knife. Place each on a square of non-stick paper and place them, not touching, in a steaming basket. Cover the buns and leave 15 minutes to rise.

Dilute red food colouring with water, dip a new toothbrush in it, and with a flick of the thumb along the bristles, spray colour onto one side of peach for blush. Steam for 12 to 15 minutes. Turn off the heat, and wait for 1 minute before uncovering the buns.

# pineapple tarts

makes about 36

**Filling**
1 x 850 g (1 lb 12 oz) can crushed
    pineapple pieces
1½ cups sugar
1 stick cinnamon
2 tablespoons semolina
2 tablespoons pineapple syrup

**Pastry**
2 cups plain flour
125 g (4 oz) unsalted butter
½ cup caster sugar
1 egg yolk
1 teaspoon vanilla essence

Drain pineapple, reserving the syrup. Put the drained pineapple into a heavy pan and add sugar and cinnamon. Bring this to the boil and stir it over a medium heat for 15 minutes.

Mix the semolina with 2 tablespoons of pineapple syrup, stirring out any lumps. Add the mixture to the pan and stir constantly for 15 minutes or until the mixture is thick. Allow it to cool completely.

Sift the flour into a bowl. Cut the butter into small pieces and add to flour, rubbing in lightly with the fingertips. Add the caster sugar and mix through. Beat the egg yolk and vanilla with 2 tablespoons of iced water. Pour this over the flour and mix gently to make a soft dough, adding an extra tablespoon of water if necessary. Wrap the dough in plastic and chill it for 30 minutes.

Preheat oven to moderately hot, 190°C (375°F). Roll out pastry thinly, cut with small round cutter and line tart cases. Fill with pineapple, decorate tops with strips of pastry or make decorative edge. Place the tart cases on a baking tray and bake for 15 minutes or until the pastry is golden. Cool and store in an airtight container until serving time.

# love cake

| | | | |
|---|---|---|---|
| 250 | g (8 oz) medium fine semolina | 2 | tablespoons rose water or |
| 5 | eggs | | ¼ teaspoon rose essence |
| 1 | cup caster sugar | 2 | teaspoons lime rind, finely |
| 30 | g (1 oz) unsalted butter, | | chopped |
| | softened | 1 | teaspoon ground cardamom |
| 125 | ml (4 fl oz) evaporated milk | 1 | teaspoon freshly grated nutmeg |
| 2 | tablespoons each honey and | 250 | g (8 oz) raw cashews |
| | brandy | | |

Line a deep 23 cm (9 inch) square cake tin with baking paper and preheat the oven to slow, 120°C (250°F).

Toast the semolina in a dry pan, stirring constantly, until golden. Turn out onto a tray to cool. In large bowl beat 3 eggs and 2 yolks with sugar until they are thick and light. Add all the remaining ingredients and mix well. Whisk the remaining 2 egg whites until they are stiff, fold them into the mixture.

Pour the mixture into the tin and bake it for one hour. After an hour, protect the top with foil and continue baking about one hour longer or until brown and firm enough not to wobble when the pan is shaken. The skewer test does not apply here, as the cake should be sticky in the centre. Cool the cake and cut into small serving squares.

# bibingka royal

3 large eggs
¾ cup caster sugar
185 ml (6 fl oz) canned coconut milk
4 tablespoons melted butter
2 cups of self-raising flour
3 tablespoons finely grated
   cheese
freshly grated coconut, optional

Beat the eggs well in a large bowl. Reserve one tablespoonful of the sugar for sprinkling on at the end. Add the remaining sugar gradually to the eggs, beating them until thick and light. Mix 125 ml (4 fl oz) of water with coconut milk and stir it in with half the melted butter. Fold in the flour and mix well.

Pour the mixture into a greased and floured 23 cm (9 inch) square tin and bake it in a preheated moderate oven, 180°C (350°F), until the cake is golden and well risen (20 to 25 minutes). Remove the cake from the oven and brush the top with the remaining melted butter, sprinkling with cheese and the reserved tablespoon of caster sugar. Cut the cake into squares and, if preferred, sprinkle with grated fresh coconut.

# coconut jelly

serves 12

- 1 tablespoon agar-agar powder
- 1 cup sugar
- 375 ml (12 fl oz) canned coconut milk

- 3 egg whites
- few drops rose, vanilla or almond essence, optional
- food colouring

Put 375 ml (12 fl oz) of water into a saucepan and sprinkle the agar-agar evenly over the
surface. Place the saucepan over a medium heat and stir until it boils and the agar-agar is completely dissolved. Add ¾ cup of sugar, stirring to dissolve. Remove the pan from the heat and stir in the coconut milk.

Whisk the egg whites in a clean, dry bowl until they are stiff. Add the remaining sugar and
whisk until the mixture is thick and glossy. Stir this briskly into the coconut jelly while it is still lukewarm. Stir until no lumps of egg white remain. The mixture may be coloured a delicate shade of pink or orange. Pour it into a square dish rinsed in cold water and leave it to set. Cut it into large diamond shapes when firm.

# coconut cake

makes 1 large cake

- finely grated flesh of two coconuts or 3 cups desiccated coconut
- 5 eggs separated
- 2¼ cups caster sugar
- 2 cups fine rice flour
- 1 cup self-raising flour

- 3 teaspoons baking powder
- 1 teaspoon ground cardamom
- ¼ teaspoon ground cloves
- 1 tablespoon rose water or ½ teaspoon rose essence
- 1 cup finely chopped raw cashews

Line a 25 cm (10 inch) square cake pan with baking paper. Preheat oven to moderately
slow, 160° C (325°F).

Put the fresh coconut into the blender with 1½ cups of water and blend until very fine.
If using desiccated coconut, increase water to 3 cups. Using an electric mixer, beat egg yolks, ¼ cup of the blended coconut and 2 cups of the caster sugar until light and creamy. Add remaining coconut and beat well.

Sift dry ingredients and ground spices and stir into the mixture with flavouring and nuts.
Beat egg whites until stiff, add reserved ¼ cup sugar and beat until glossy. Fold into batter and pour into prepared tin. Bake for 1 hour 15 minutes or until golden brown and a fine skewer inserted in the centre comes out clean. If it browns too quickly, cover the top with foil and cook until done. Cool before cutting into squares.

# almond biscuits

makes 16 to 20

125 g (4 oz) lard, softened
½ cup caster sugar
1 teaspoon almond essence
1½ cups plain flour
16 – 20 blanched almond halves
1 egg yolk

Beat the lard with the caster sugar and almond essence until it is soft and creamy. Stir in the flour a little at a time. Take level tablespoons of dough and shape into flat rounds of about 5 cm (2 inches) in diameter. Place these on a baking tray lined with non-stick paper and press half an almond in the centre of each. Brush the tops of biscuits with egg yolk beaten with a tablespoon of cold water.

Bake the biscuits in a preheated slow oven, 150–160°C (300–325°F), for 30 minutes or until they are pale golden. Leave them on the tray to cool slightly, then lift them carefully onto a wire rack until completely cold. Store in airtight container.

**Note** Whole almonds my be easily split by bringing them to the boil in a little water, draining, then splitting.

UR WISDOM W
ND A
TAKE A POSITIVE APPROACH.
BE PATIENT - SUCCESS AWAITS.
YOU HAVE A SECRET ADM

# fortune cookies

*You can write your own 'fortunes'. Have these written on strips of paper before you begin cooking.*

makes about 12

2 egg whites
⅓ cup caster sugar
2 tablespoons cornflour
2 tablespoons plain flour
½ teaspoon vanilla or ¼ teaspoon almond essence
1 teaspoon peanut oil

Preheat the oven to moderate, 180°C (350°F). Brush the baking trays with oil and dust them with extra cornflour, tapping the trays on a hard surface to remove excess cornflour. On each tray mark two circles with the rim of a teacup.

Beat the egg whites until they are frothy, add the sugar and mix well. Sift the cornflour and flour together and stir it into the mixture with the flavouring essence and peanut oil. Drop 2 teaspoons of the batter in each circle and spread it with a spatula or the back of a spoon. Bake the cookies for about 8 minutes or until they are pale golden. As soon as they are cooked, remove one cookie from a tray, place a fortune inside and fold it over to enclose the slip of paper. Quickly bend the cookie over the edge of a bowl to give it a twist. Repeat this with the other cookies. If they become too cool and firm, return the tray to the oven briefly to soften them. Cool the cookies completely on a wire rack and store them in an airtight container. Use within a few days.

**Note** Photograph of fortune cookies is on page 85 with the almond biscuits

# sauces & dips

# sweet chilli sauce

makes about
750 ml (24 fl oz)

125 g (4 oz) red chillies or ¼ cup
    chilli powder
500 ml (16 fl oz) white vinegar
1½ cups sugar
250 g (8 oz) sultanas

1 tablespoon chopped garlic
1 tablespoon finely grated fresh
    ginger
1½ teaspoons salt or to taste
    bottled tomato ketchup,
    optional

Wear gloves to remove the seeds from the chillies. Chop the chillies roughly and put them into a blender with 250 ml (8 fl oz) vinegar, blending until smooth. In a non-aluminium saucepan, combine all the ingredients and bring it to the boil. Cook the sauce over a low heat until the sultanas are very soft, about 25 minutes. Cool, then purée the mixture in the blender. Taste the sauce. If the chillies are hot it may need toning down to your taste with bottled tomato ketchup.

# sweet -sour sauce

makes 250 ml
(8 fl oz)

125 ml (4 fl oz) white vinegar
125 ml (4 fl oz) canned pineapple
    juice
2 tablespoons sugar

1 tablespoon tomato ketchup
½ teaspoon salt
1 teaspoon cornflour

Combine all the ingredients except the cornflour in a small non-aluminium saucepan and bring the mixture to the boil. Mix the cornflour to a smooth cream with a tablespoon of cold water, stir this into the pan until it boils and thickens.

# tamarind chutney

makes 185 ml
(6 fl oz)

3 tablespoons dried tamarind
pulp
½ teaspoon salt
3 teaspoons sugar
1 teaspoon ground cummin

½ teaspoon ground fennel
2 teaspoons finely grated fresh
ginger
pinch of chilli powder, optional

Put the tamarind in a bowl and pour over 185 (6 fl oz) of boiling water. Leave this until cool, then knead and squeeze the pulp until it has dissolved. Strain this through a fine nylon sieve, pushing all the pulp through. Discard the seeds. Add the remaining ingredients to the pulp, taste and adjust seasonings to taste.

# mint or coriander dip with yoghurt

makes about
375 ml (12 fl oz)

90 ml 3 fl oz) lemon juice
2 tablespoons water
1 firmly packed cup mint or
coriander leaves
1 cup spring onions, roughly
chopped (include leaves)

2 fresh green chillies
1 teaspoon salt
3 teaspoons sugar
1 teaspoon garam masala
125 ml (4 fl oz) thick yoghurt

Put the lemon juice and water in a blender and add all the other ingredients except the yoghurt. Blend the mixture to a smooth purée. Turn it into a bowl and gently stir in the yoghurt. Cover and chill until required.

# crunchy *peanut sauce*

*A sauce which will keep, refrigerated, for weeks in an airtight jar only if you hide it well — it's good enough to eat on a spoon, on crackers, or in sandwiches. Add coconut milk or water as needed. Remember, however, to taste and adjust salt and lemon juice and, if you are a chilli lover, even add a splash of chilli sauce to make the flavour interesting. Too many cooks serve a peanut sauce which is too sweet, has none of the gutsy garlic and chilli, and detracts from whatever it is served with.*

**makes 2 cups sauce base**

- ½ cup peanut oil
- 2 teaspoons dried garlic flakes
- 3 tablespoons dried onion flakes
- 2 large dried chillies
- 1 teaspoon dried shrimp paste

- 1 tablespoon soy sauce
- 1 tablespoon lemon juice
- 375 g (12 oz) crunchy peanut butter
- 1 tablespoon palm or brown sugar

In a wok, heat oil and gently fry the garlic until pale golden. Lift out with a wire mesh strainer and drain on paper towels. Fry onion flakes in the same manner, taking care not to burn them. Lift out and drain. Fry chillies whole until they darken but do not burn. Drain. When cool, remove stems and shake out seeds. Crumble and set aside with fried garlic and onion. Fry shrimp paste in oil that remains, crushing it with the frying spoon as it cooks. Add soy sauce and lemon juice and mix well. Turn off heat, add peanut butter and stir. When completely cold, add sugar, garlic, onion and chillies. Bottle and refrigerate.

To serve, the sauce base should be thinned with an equal amount of diluted coconut milk — ¾ cup of each will yield enough sauce to serve 6. This sauce also makes a tasty vegetarian dish (gado-gado) when poured over mixed raw and boiled vegetables and hard boiled eggs.

# pepper and coriander paste

**makes about 250 ml (8 fl oz)**

- 1 tablespoon chopped garlic
- 2 teaspoons salt
- 1 tablespoon whole black peppercorns

- 2 cups coarsely chopped fresh coriander, including roots
- 2 tablespoons lemon juice

Crush the garlic and the salt to a smooth paste. Roast the peppercorns in a dry pan for a minute or two. Finely chop the coriander roots, leaves and stems. Mix all the ingredients with the lemon juice and grind in a blender, adding a little water if necessary.

# glossary

**Annatto seeds**
Used for colouring and flavouring Filipino food. Also known as achuete (pronounced ash-way-tay).

**Besan**
Chickpea flour, sold at Indian shops and many health food stores. It has a strong, distinctive flavour and the nearest substitute is pea flour, but this must be sifted through a very fine sieve as it is usually much coarser.

**Chillies**
Fresh chillies should be handled with care as the volatile oils can cause much discomfort. Small chillies are hotter than large ones. Wear gloves when handling. It is possible to buy fresh chopped chillies in jars which may be substituted, and also Sambal Oelek (Ulek) which is a mixture of fresh chillies and salt. Or there is Tabasco Pepper Sauce. Use 1 teaspoon in place of each hot chilli.

**Garam masala**
Essential in Indian dishes. Roast separately until fragrant—2 tablespoons coriander seeds, 1 tablespoon cummin seeds, 2 teaspoons whole black peppercorns, 1 teaspoon cardamom seeds (remove from pods), 2 cinnamon sticks and 10 whole cloves. Grind as finely as possible and mix in half a nutmeg, finely grated. Store airtight.

**Kecap manis**
Thick, sweet soy sauce.

**Maldive fish pieces**
Used to add flavour to almost every Sri Lankan dish. It may be purchased already pounded or crushed, but often needs further pulverising in a blender or mortar and pestle.

**Melinjo crackers**
Parchment coloured discs made from the flattened and dried seeds of the fruit of a tree native to tropical Asia. Deep fry a few at a time in hot oil, drain on paper towels and sprinkle lightly with salt.

**Mirin**
Japanese sweet rice wine, used only for cooking. Sweet sherry may be substituted, though flavour is not the same.

**Nam prik pao**
A thick, hot and sweet chilli and dried shrimp Thai relish cooked in oil. Sold in jars in Asian stores.

**Nuoc cham**
A typical Vietnamese dipping sauce made from the juice and pulp of a lime, 2 tablespoons each of fish sauce, water and white sugar, a little crushed garlic and hot chilli, seeded and sliced

**Sev**
A fine noodle made from chick pea flour which has been deep fried until crisp. Sold in packets at Indian grocers.

**Shiitake mushroom**
Dried Chinese or Japanese mushrooms are the Shiitake variety. Dried European mushrooms are no substitute.

**Shrimp, dried**
Sold loose by weight, or in plastic packets. They should be salmon pink in colour and will keep for months, preferably in the refrigerator. Usually soaked before use.

**Sweetened lotus nut paste or black bean paste**
Sold in cans at Chinese grocery shops. Used as a filling in steamed buns or Chinese pastries.

**Tamarind**
Gives acidity to many dishes. It is sold dried, puréed or instant. the dried pulp has the truest flavour.

# index